D0016403

BABE RUTH

BY ART BERKE

AN IMPACT BIOGRAPHY I FRANKLIN WATTS
NEW YORK I LONDON I TORONTO I SYDNEY I 1988

Photographs courtesy of:
National Baseball Library, Cooperstown, N.Y.: pp. 2,
13 (AP/Wide World Photos), 19, 21, 25, 34, 43, 50,
59, 64, 74 (Carl Seid), 83 (AP/Wide World Photos),
89 (Esquire Magazine); UPI/Bettmann Newsphotos: pp.
58 66, 76, 77, 85, 93, 96, 98, 100, 102.

Library of Congress Cataloging-in-Publication Data

Berke, Art.
Babe Ruth / by Art Berke.
p.   cm.—(An Impact biography)
Bibliography: p.
Includes index.
Summary: Presents the life and career of George Herman Ruth,
perhaps the most talented and popular player in baseball history.
ISBN 0-531-10472-9
1. Ruth, Babe, 1895-1948—Juvenile literature. 2. Baseball
players—United States—Biography—Juvenile literature. [1. Ruth,
Babe, 1895-1948. 2. Baseball players.] I. Title.
GV865.R8B47   1988
796.357′092′4—dc19
[B]
[92]   87-27366 CIP AC

TO MY MOTHER AND FATHER,
EVE AND SEYMOUR BERKE,
WHOSE RUTHIAN EFFORTS
GAVE ME THE CHANCE
TO PURSUE MY DREAMS

The author would like
to thank the staff of
the National Baseball Hall
of Fame and Museum and
National Baseball Library
in Cooperstown, New York,
for their cooperation
and guidance

Contents

THE BEST THERE
EVER WAS

Babe Ruth was simply the best there ever was. Maybe Ty Cobb was a better overall hitter, Willie Mays and Joe DiMaggio could do more things, and Cy Young and Walter Johnson were better pitchers. But, all in all, in the history of baseball, Ruth stands above the rest.

His accomplishments on the field were monumental, such as his 714 home runs, a .342 lifetime batting average, and a .671 winning percentage as a pitcher. But mere statistics don't come close to telling the story of George Herman Ruth. During the "Golden Age" of sports, in the 1920s, Babe was baseball's biggest drawing card and America's most beloved sports hero. His awesome power, fun-loving nature, childlike enthusiasm, love of kids, barrel-chested physique, and flair for the dramatic all contributed to his larger-than-life image. For all of this, and other factors that are probably beyond explanation, the "Bambino's" legend endures today despite the passing of the years and the fact that many of his records have been broken.

Generations of Americans have been touched by the Ruth magic. This includes those who played with and

against him during his heyday with the Boston Red Sox and New York Yankees as well as fans who either flocked through the turnstiles to watch him perform or have read or heard about his heroic exploits.

Fred Lindstrom, a member of baseball's Hall of Fame, once pointed out that baseball's existence is a tribute to Ruth. Hall of Fame pitcher Ted Lyons observed that Babe was the only player who could draw 30,000 fans just to watch batting practice. Front office executive and manager Ed Barrow, who was with Ruth in both Boston and New York, remarked that, in his opinion, there never has been and never will be anybody like him. Teammate and manager Bob Shawkey commented that he never knew anyone who didn't like Babe. And Japanese soldiers in World War II even shouted, "To hell with Babe Ruth!" as the ultimate insult to American GIs.[1]

Of all the words spoken about the Babe, perhaps former teammate and close friend Waite Hoyt said it best years ago:

Will there ever be another Ruth? Don't be silly! Oh, sure, somebody may come along some day who will hit more than 60 home runs in a season [Roger Maris hit 61 in 1961] or more than 714 in a career [Hank Aaron clouted a record total of 755], but that won't make him another Ruth.

The Bambino's appeal was to the emotions. Don't tell me about Ruth; I've seen what he did to people. I've seen them—fans—driving miles in open wagons through the prairies of Oklahoma to see him in exhibition games as we headed north in the spring. I've seen them: kids, men, women, worshippers all, hoping to get his famous name on a torn, dirty piece of paper, or hoping to get recognition when they said, "Hi'ya, Babe."

He never let them down; not once! He was the greatest crowd pleaser of them all! It wasn't so much that he hit home runs, it was how he hit them and the circumstances under which he hit them. Another Ruth? Never![2]

Babe Ruth's story is about a youngster's love affair with baseball. It's the story of how an incorrigible youth from a Baltimore home for boys grew up to revolutionize the game of baseball with his exceptional athletic skill and flamboyant style—and how he became the idol of millions. It is truly an example of the American dream.

As a man, Ruth was far from perfect. He had little discipline and an enormous appetite for food, alcohol, and cigars, caroused off the field, and was a reckless driver. This book, however, pays more heed to Ruth's heroics between the white lines of the baseball diamond and the impact Ruth continues to have as one of America's premier sports heroes.

Chapter 2

A STAR IN
THE MAKING

On February 6, 1895, in a small room on the second floor of his grandfather's house on the Baltimore, Maryland, waterfront, George Herman Ruth, Jr., was born.

Little George, as he was first called by his family, was the oldest of eight children born to George and Katherine Schamberger Ruth, whose ancestors were primarily German. Because of various health problems, only one of the seven Ruth children born after George lived to maturity. This was George's sister, Mamie, who was born when he was five.

Growing up in the rough waterfront neighborhood was not easy for the young boy. His mother and father tended to the family saloon and grocery, where they also lived, and George was left alone much of the time. He was a frequent absentee from school and ran around with an undesirable group of boys who got into all kinds of mischief, including drinking, stealing, and chewing tobacco.

"I spent most of the first seven years of my life living over my father's saloon," George once said. "When I wasn't living over it, I was living in it, studying the rough

George Ruth as a young child

talk of the longshoremen, merchant sailors, roustabouts and waterfront bums. When I wasn't living in it, I was living in the neighborhood streets. I had a rotten start and it took me a long time to get my bearings."[1]

A few months after his seventh birthday, George was labeled a juvenile delinquent and was sent to the St. Mary's Industrial School for Boys. The years he spent at St. Mary's, off and on from ages seven to nineteen, turned his life around.

In the early 1900s, St. Mary's Industrial School welcomed all types of boys. Although it did serve as a reform school for boys who misbehaved, it was also a haven for youngsters of virtually all backgrounds who came from broken homes or who just needed closer supervision.

When George entered St. Mary's, he was one of nearly a thousand boys who were overseen by a group of Xaverian brothers from the Catholic church. Under the tutelage of these men, the boys had to follow a strict regimen of activities that included religious instruction, academic studies, industrial training, and athletics.

Classroom work was hard for George. He seemed distracted in his studies and was not able to concentrate for long. However, he enjoyed his work at the school's tailor shop and became quite a good shirtmaker, making token wages that were put into his account at the school store. And quite frequently he would use his hard-earned money to buy things for the younger boys.

"Kids happen to like me, feel natural around me," said Ruth, who would later become known for his generosity and love of children. "I'm the same around them. It isn't just a case of giving out autographs. I've always felt cleaner after a session with kids. Wherever they've gathered they've turned my thoughts back to St. Mary's."[2]

Where George excelled the most, of course, was on the athletic field. At St. Mary's, as with the United States in general in those days, baseball was the most popular

George (center) at St. Mary's

sport, and the school was highly regarded throughout the region for its excellence on the diamond. From the moment he began playing ball, Ruth, who batted and threw left-handed, had a special feeling for the game. And from the start Brother Matthias, whom George later said was "the greatest man I've ever known,"[3] took the boy under his wing and encouraged him to take advantage of his talents.

Brother Matthias certainly must have been an exceptional human being. He was a strict disciplinarian, whose great height—6 feet 6 inches (2.3 m)—and 250-pound (114-kg) frame added to his aura. He was a fair man and universally respected, even by George, who at times was considered one of the school's biggest troublemakers. It was obvious that Matthias, who was most responsible for putting Ruth on the right track, gave George what he apparently never got from his own father—love and attention.

Under Brother Matthias's watchful eye, George began to develop his athletic prowess. He was a muscular 6 feet 2 inches (2.2 m) tall and weighed 170 pounds (77.5 kg) in his last few years at St. Mary's and was noticeably bigger than the other boys. He became the school's most prized baseball player and it was always a treat for the other youngsters when they got a chance to see George in action.

Ruth was primarily a catcher until an interesting occurrence forced him onto the pitcher's mound. One day during a ball game, George, always the boisterous one, was laughing at how poorly one of the boys was pitching. Brother Matthias took note of Ruth's behavior and, trying to teach him a lesson, said, "All right, George, you pitch."

"I never pitched in my life," George replied. "I can't pitch."

"Oh, you must know a lot about it," Brother Matthias fired back. "You know enough to know that your friend isn't any good. So go ahead out there and show us how it's done."

So, without any previous pitching experience, George tossed aside his catcher's equipment, borrowed a fielder's glove, and walked toward the mound.

"I didn't even know how to stand on the rubber, or how to throw a curve or even how to get the ball over the plate," George later admitted. "Yet, as I took the position I felt, somehow, as if I had been born out there and this was kind of a home for me. It seemed the most natural thing in the world to start pitching—and to start striking out batters."[4]

George Ruth, who had already become the school's best hitter, was now on his way to becoming its best pitcher as well. And when he wasn't playing at St. Mary's he was competing in games outside the school, having been given permission to leave the grounds on weekends.

George kept getting better and better, and in February of 1914, at the age of nineteen, he got his first big break in baseball. On the basis of a letter of recommendation by Brother Gilbert, the athletic director at a rival school, and several glowing "scouting reports," Jack Dunn, owner of the minor-league Baltimore Orioles, signed George up to a six-month contract for $600.

I'll never forget the day Brother Gilbert called me over and introduced me to Jack," said Ruth. "I was flabbergasted. I hadn't known about the letter, and the idea of shaking hands with a real professional baseball man was almost too much.

Jack was mighty good to me and talked for quite a while about baseball. Finally, he got me into a uniform and out in the yard. He had me pitch to him, and at the end of a half-hour, Dunn called a halt and went into the office with Brother Gilbert. Later, they called me in, and Brother Gilbert explained that Mr. Dunn thought I'd make a ballplayer and wanted me to sign a contract with the Orioles. Since I *wasn't yet of age, Brother Gilbert explained, Mr. Dunn would take out papers as my guardian and would be responsible for me when I was away from the school. . . .*[5]

I had some great moments in the years that followed that . . . but none of my later thrills ever topped the one I got that cold afternoon at St. Mary's when $600 seemed to me to be all the wealth in the world.[6]

George Ruth's days at St. Mary's finally came to an end, but in the years to come he would always have a special place in his heart for the Baltimore institution. During the 1920 season, for instance, he would arrange for the St. Mary's band to travel with the Yankees to help raise funds to rebuild school property that had been destroyed by fire the previous winter. Ruth never forgot those, such as Brother Matthias, whose love and guidance enabled him to go out on his own and do what he loved to do best—play baseball.

At nineteen years of age, George Ruth was on his way to becoming a minor-league ballplayer with the Baltimore Orioles of the International League. George's new adventure would mean more than simply the challenge of playing ball with professionals. He would be leaving his small world, consisting of St. Mary's, various playing fields around Baltimore, and the waterfront where he was born, to inhabit a much bigger universe—playing in such cities as Rochester and Buffalo, New York; Providence, Rhode Island; and Toronto and Montreal, Canada.

"The whole thing seemed like a dream to me," Ruth explained. "There were moments when I felt I sat on top of the world and moments that my stomach turned over, wondering if I could make the grade and fearful that I'd fail, and be forced to come back to St. Mary's."[7]

The Orioles were entering their fifth season under the ownership of Dunn, a former major-league pitcher. He had developed his franchise into an outstanding minor-league

*Ruth poses with members of
St. Mary's Band in 1920.*

organization and discovered a host of other players who later would make it to the big leagues, including the great pitcher Lefty Grove. But at this time Dunn was facing a sizable threat to his team's status in the league as well as their standing in the community.

Dunn's problems were due to the formation of a third major league, the Federal League, which included a team in Baltimore (the Terrapins) principally owned by the popular Ned Hanlon, who managed the original Baltimore Orioles team, an outstanding major-league club in the 1890s. Dunn knew he had his work cut out for him, battling both a major-league franchise and the popularity of Hanlon. He tried to combat these overwhelming odds by building the finest ballclub possible. Ruth, both a promising young pitcher and a native of Baltimore, could help him accomplish this.

A few days after he said goodbye to all of his friends at St. Mary's, George set out for spring training in Fayetteville, North Carolina. Buckets of rain greeted George and his teammates when they got off the train there. (Airplane travel for ballplayers was decades away.) Ruth would have to wait a few days for his first game.

The day of Ruth's professional debut finally arrived on March 7, 1914. Ruth started the seven-inning intrasquad game playing shortstop, a position he had played only briefly at St. Mary's. In the game he hit a long home run that was the talk of the town for years to come and pitched two impressive innings. It wasn't long before the newspapers began to spread the word back in Baltimore that their native son was something special.

"Ruth has all the earmarks of a good ballplayer," Dunn boasted. "He hits like a fiend and seems to be at home at any position, despite the fact that he is a left-hander. He's the most promising young ballplayer I've ever seen."[8]

Ruth was indeed performing like a professional on the field. But off the field he was still an immature boy and enjoyed riding up and down the hotel elevator and playing with the kids of Fayetteville more than spending time with his own teammates, who didn't include him in their closely knit circle. The Orioles' new star also gained his legendary nickname that spring. Seeing how young and innocent George was, the rest of the Orioles began to call him "Dunn's Babe," and thus the most famous nickname in sports was coined.

Babe's reputation as baseball's newest star really grew during a series of spring exhibition games with some of the major leagues' strongest clubs. In his first performance, against the world champion Philadelphia Athletics, Ruth pitched the Orioles to a 6–2 victory. And, in subsequent triumphs over the Phillies and Dodgers, he impressed everyone who saw him play.

Following a successful stint at training camp, Babe was now ready to make his official regular season debut. On April 22, in the Orioles' second game, Ruth appeared against the Buffalo Bisons in Baltimore. Although he had the usual rookie jitters, he was masterful on the mound, hurling a 6–0, six-hit shutout. To top it off, he also hit two singles. In that same game there was a second baseman on the Bisons team by the name of Joe McCarthy; this was the same Joe McCarthy who would manage Ruth in New York nearly twenty years later.

During those first weeks with the Orioles, Babe became an instant hit wherever he played, both as a pitcher and a slugger. He was given several increases in salary and was quickly becoming a very popular figure in Baltimore. But the Orioles, despite their first place standing, were drawing small crowds and as a result were feeling the financial pinch created by the success of the Terrapins (who even offered Babe a bundle to leave the Orioles and play for their team).

Ultimately, Dunn had to sell his best players to avoid a total collapse. At the beginning of July, Babe, standout pitcher Ernie Shore, and veteran catcher Ben Egan were sold to the American League Boston Red Sox club, whose owner, Joe Lannin, paid approximately $25,000 for the three players. Babe, who had played at St. Mary's on a championship team named after the Red Sox, was now going to play for the real, major-league team.

Chapter 3

RUTH OF
THE RED SOX

The major leagues! George Herman Ruth of Baltimore became Babe Ruth of the Boston Red Sox, world champions in 1912 and a few years later still one of baseball's most star-studded teams, with the likes of future Hall of Fame outfielders Tris Speaker and Harry Hooper, plus all-time greats such as pitcher Smokey Joe Wood and outfielder Duffy Lewis. Still just nineteen and unaccustomed to the new world around him, the Babe Ruth who would later become a household name was still light-years away. Said Hooper, who along with Speaker and Lewis formed one of the greatest outfields of all time:

Babe joined us in the middle of 1914. . . . He was a left-handed pitcher then, and a good one. He had never been anywhere, didn't know anything about manners or how to behave . . . just a big, overgrown green pea. You probably remember him with that big belly later on. But that wasn't there in 1914. George was 6-2 [2.2 m], weighed 198 pounds [90 kg], all of it muscle. He had a slim waist, huge biceps, no self-discipline and not much education—not so much different from a lot of other nineteen-year-old would-be ballplayers. Except for two things: He could eat more than anyone else, and he could hit a baseball further . . . But sometimes I still can't believe what I saw: this nineteen-year-old kid, crude, poorly educated, only lightly brushed by the social veneer we call civilization, gradually transformed into the idol of American youth and the symbol of baseball the world over—a man loved by more people with an intensity of feeling that perhaps has never been equaled before or since. I saw a man transformed into a god.[1]

When Babe joined the Red Sox, the club was in sixth place (out of eight teams) and destined to finish second, behind the powerful Philadelphia A's. Although he would soon have an enormous impact on the fortunes of the team, Babe did little at first. He won his initial major-league game, a 4–3 decision over Cleveland, but he didn't get much chance to play for manager Bill Carrigan. Then, in mid-August, just weeks after his arrival at Boston's Fenway Park, he was sent down to the Providence Grays, the Red Sox's top minor-league club, to help that team in their quest for the International League pennant.

Although he received the same salary, which had risen to $3,500, Babe was not happy with the club's edict. He felt he had done his apprenticeship in the minors and was ready for full-time major-league duty. Despite his reservations, however, Ruth soon adjusted to the Providence club, which was managed by colorful "Wild Bill" Donovan, a former major-league hurler who helped Babe make the transition from thrower to pitcher.

"I used to buzz them past the letters, too," Donovan told Ruth. "It was a lot of fun. But if you want to last in this game as a pitcher, you've got to remember your arm is your best friend. Strikeouts count for outs in the box score, but those other outs at first base or the outfield count just as much in retiring the side."[2]

It didn't take long for Ruth to get his chance to help the Grays. Two days after he put on the uniform, the team hosted first-place Rochester in a crucial four-game series. After a Providence victory in the opener, which moved the Grays into the league lead, Babe pitched well in the second game, gaining a 5–4 triumph. A few days later in Rochester, with Providence back in second place, Ruth and another pitcher, Carl Mays, won both ends of a doubleheader to put the Grays back in the lead.

The Ruth-Mays pitching combination continued to be successful, with an impressive string of victories down the stretch. This included Babe's 9–0 one-hitter at Toronto, a game in which Ruth also hit a homer, his first and only minor-league home run.

Behind the pitching of Ruth and Mays, who later would become a teammate of Babe's in both Boston and New York, Providence eventually clinched the league's pennant. Shortly after that, Ruth was called back to Boston, where he claimed another pitching victory and recorded his first major-league hit, a double off of the Yankees' Leonard "King" Cole.

It might not have been exactly what he expected, having played in three different cities, but Babe's first year in pro ball certainly gave the baseball world a glimpse of his coming greatness.

The year 1914 was a memorable one for Ruth in another respect. After the season was over, he married Helen Woodford, a Boston waitress. Although the couple would begin their lives together happily enough, and even take into their home an adopted daughter, Dorothy, their marriage would not be a successful one. It would be marked by numerous conflicts and separations, and after 1925 Babe and Helen would rarely see each other.

During that first winter together, the newlyweds spent the off-season with Ruth's father in Baltimore. (His mother had died a few years earlier.) Babe worked with his dad in the family saloon. Over the years Ruth would continue to visit his father from time to time, until 1918, when the elder Ruth would be killed in a barroom fight.

* * * * *

From the moment the 1915 season began it was obvious that Babe would be a major contributor to the Red Sox fortunes. Although he was still raw and undisciplined, Ruth was proving to be an extraordinary talent. He showed a fierce competitive spirit, a keen instinct for the game, and with the help of manager Bill Carrigan, he learned to mix an outstanding fastball with a devastating curve. His first full major-league season was an unqualified success.

Ruth wasn't the only member of the Red Sox to shine in 1915, as the club established itself as baseball's best team. The Sox won 101 games, edging out Ty Cobb's Detroit Tigers to win the American League pennant. They then defeated the Philadelphia Phillies, the National League champions, in five games to capture the World Series.

Although he was strictly a pitcher in those days, except for occasional pinch-hitting duties (because of the Red Sox's deep pitching staff, Babe's only World Series appearance that year was as a pinch hitter against the great pitcher Grover Cleveland Alexander), Babe was always proud of his hitting. Even with his limited plate appearances he hit four home runs that season, only three behind the league leader (home runs were far less common in those days than they are today). The first, his initial major-league home run, was a memorable one. It was an upper deck shot to right field on May 6, off of Yankee pitcher Jack Warhop at New York's Polo Grounds, the same location Babe would later send dozens of home runs to as a member of the Yankees in the early 1920s.

Ruth, for all his maturity as an athlete, was going through considerable growing pains in his adjustment to the outside world. His casual attitude and newfound free-

Babe, early in his career, pitching for the Boston Red Sox

dom from the restrictions at St. Mary's led him to ignore virtually all of the team's rules, including staying out until all hours. This infuriated Bill Carrigan. And perhaps because he grew up poor, he didn't seem able to hold onto money. He became a lavish spender, needing to have the biggest and best of everything (such as cars), probably to compensate for what he lacked as a child. This was a problem that would remain with Ruth all his life.

Overall, however, 1915 was quite a season for Babe. He proved he was a big leaguer, played on a world championship team, and with a World Series share of nearly $4,000 was making more money than he ever thought possible. Probably because it was his first championship and he felt Carrigan was the best manager he ever played for, Ruth always claimed that the 1915 Red Sox were one of his favorite teams.

* * * * *

During the next two years, both baseball and the Red Sox underwent significant changes. In 1916, the Federal League folded, bringing the player-bidding war to an abrupt end. Before the following season, a financially strapped Joe Lannin sold the Sox to Harry Frazee, a well-known show business promoter. Boston second baseman Jack Barry became the club's manager, replacing the retired Bill Carrigan.

These were also unsettling times for the United States. World War I, which had erupted in Europe in 1914, finally began to affect the United States, and the country entered the conflict in 1917. Even though baseball players were safe (Babe, being a married man, was exempt in any case), it was only a matter of time before they would be affected.

Despite all the changes around him, Babe clearly established himself as the ace of the Boston pitching staff, as well as the best lefthander in the league, reaching a salary of $5,000 (very good in those days). And he was a major reason why the Red Sox won their second straight

World Series in 1916, and finished a respectable second to the powerful Chicago White Sox in 1917.

To give an example of his abilities as a pitcher in that period, Ruth was enormously successful when he went head-to-head with the man many considered to be the game's best pitcher, Walter "Big Train" Johnson of the Washington Senators, who led the league in victories from 1913 to 1916 and in 1918 and 1924. In 1916, Ruth won four of four decisions against the "Big Train" and captured six of nine decisions against Johnson in his career.

Perhaps the finest moment of Ruth's early career was during the 1916 World Series against the Brooklyn Dodgers, which Boston won four games to one. All things considered, it was not one of the most memorable series, but the second game, which featured Babe's heroics on the mound, still ranks as the longest (in terms of innings) in Fall Classic history and one of the most exciting ever.

After Red Sox pitcher Ernie Shore posted a thrilling 6-5 win in Game 1, Ruth faced the Dodgers and pitcher Sherry Smith in the second contest at Boston. The Dodgers got on the scoreboard first, as Brooklyn centerfielder Hy Myers hit an inside-the-park home run in the top of the first inning. In the third, the Red Sox tied the game on a Ruth ground-out to third base. For the next eleven innings, as a result of spectacular pitching on both sides, it was a stalemate until Boston pushed across the winning run in the bottom of the fourteenth. Babe was superb in his fourteen-inning performance, allowing only six hits in the game and pitching near-perfect ball from the ninth inning on.

An interesting event happened during the early part of 1917 that has become a fascinating part of baseball lore. Babe was losing his temper frequently and having his share of skirmishes with umpires. On June 23, he started a game against the Washington Senators at Fenway Park. After walking the first batter, he became so enraged at home plate umpire Brick Owens that he struck him. As a result, he was thrown out of the game, fined, and suspended for ten days.

Ernie Shore came on in relief of Ruth. The next batter, who reached on a walk, was immediately thrown out at second base, and Shore proceeded to retire the next twenty-six batters. It was only the fifth perfect game in major-league history. And it was becoming apparent to all that whenever Babe Ruth was involved, it was going to become a memorable occasion.

HIGHLIGHTS AND KEY STATISTICS: 1914–1917

In his first year as a professional ballplayer, Babe won 22 games for Baltimore and Providence in the International League and showed promise when called upon as a hitter as well. His outstanding pitching enabled the Orioles to get off to a big lead and later helped the Grays to the league pennant. Ruth also won his first 2 major-league games as a member of the Boston Red Sox.

In 1915, Babe compiled an impressive 18–8 record, struck out 112 batters, and finished the season with a respectable 2.44 earned run average (ERA).

During the 1916 season, Ruth had a 23–12 won-lost record and an impressive 1.75 ERA. He ranked first among American League pitchers in ERA and shutouts, tied for second in the number of wins and innings pitched, and was third in winning percentage and strikeouts.

Babe got off to an outstanding 10–1 start in 1917 and finished the season with a 24–13 record, a fine 2.01 ERA, and 128 strikeouts—the league's fifth highest total.

Chapter 4

THE GREAT EXPERIMENT

The 1918 season was a pivotal one for Babe Ruth. His hitting, up until then exhibited only during the pitcher's normal "every fourth day" schedule, was becoming the talk of the American League. Ruth himself was emerging as the fan favorite throughout the circuit. Although there had always been some talk about switching Babe to everyday status, it was finally about to become a reality.

Tough-minded Ed Barrow, a former major-league manager and most recently the president of the International League, was named the new Red Sox manager, replacing Jack Barry. Barry, like Duffy Lewis, standout hurler Dutch Leonard, and others, had been called into the war effort. Barrow would find himself at odds with Ruth for many years to come in Boston and later in New York as the Yankee general manager. But it was he who ultimately made the decision to turn Ruth into a full-time slugger.

With so many key Red Sox in the service, it seemed logical for the club to utilize Ruth's potent bat on a more regular basis, to strengthen the offense as well as to attract fans. But even Barrow resisted at first, saying, "I'd be the laughingstock of baseball if I changed the best left-hander in the game into an outfielder."[1]

At the beginning of May, however, Barrow made his move. He asked Ruth if he would continue pitching and play in the field on his off days. Ruth said he would try, and before long he was playing either first base or the outfield.

The move quickly paid dividends, as Babe socked eleven home runs by June, a figure only three American Leaguers had previously reached during a full season. On several occasions Ruth won ballgames with his extraordinary slugging.

Ruth soon began to relish his role as a hitter and expressed a desire to give up his pitching career. He was so determined, in fact, that he left the team for two days in early July, threatening to play for a shipyard team that had assured him that he could play for them every day in the field.

Upon his return, and for the remainder of the season, shortened to Labor Day because of the need for players to contribute to the war effort and also because of dwindling attendance, Ruth did double duty. As the leading offensive producer, as well as one of the pitching stalwarts, Ruth was a major reason the Red Sox captured the AL title in 1918 and went on to win their third World Series in four years, beating the Chicago Cubs four games to two.

Ruth was superb in the Fall Classic. He shut out the Cubs in Game 1, hurling a 1–0 six-hitter, and won Game 4, 3–2. Babe also set a World Series record of 29 2/3 consecutive scoreless innings, which he had begun in the 1916 World Series. That particular milestone of consecutive scoreless innings was not broken until more than four decades later, when Whitey Ford of the New York Yankees surpassed it in 1961. Ruth said that this was one of his proudest accomplishments in baseball.

Babe always had trouble remembering faces and names, prompting him to call other players "Kid," "Doc,"

"Pal," or anything else but their real names. Before the beginning of the series opener, Barrow was going over the Chicago hitters and made a particular note of Cub outfielder Les Mann.

"The man is tough against lefthanders, Babe," he said to Ruth, who was the starting pitcher. "Any time he comes up in a pinch, I want you to be careful. In fact, it won't do any harm to dust him off a bit, for he takes a heavy toehold on the plate."

As the game proceeded, Babe thought he had carried out Barrow's orders. However, the man he plunked was not Mann but Max Flack, a lefthanded batter. When Ruth got back to the dugout, he approached Barrow.

"I guess I took care of that Mann guy for you," Babe boasted. Barrow was beside himself. "Babe, you wouldn't know General Grant if he walked up with a bat," the manager shouted.[2]

With the exception of seventeen pitching appearances (nine wins) in 1919 and a few isolated games throughout the years, Babe ended his pitching career with that extraordinary World Series. He might have ranked as the greatest pitcher of all time if he had remained a hurler. As it stands, he won ninety-four games with 488 strikeouts, a lifetime ERA of 2.28, two twenty-plus victory seasons, and a 3–0 mark in series play. That's a career for most, but for Ruth it was just part of the story.

* * * * *

Babe's pitching success and the further promise of his "Ruthian" batting prowess gave him true celebrity status. He was being greeted on and off the field with wild enthu-

In Boston, Babe was becoming as well-known for his hitting as he was for his pitching ability.

siasm. And, despite his nocturnal escapades and lack of culture, he was a hit in social circles as well. Ruth, who needed to be around people all the time, was in his glory.

Early in the 1919 season, Ruth became a full-fledged leftfielder, predicting that he'd win more games playing every day in the outfield than pitching every fourth day. He was certainly ready for full-time hitting duty, but was baseball ready for him?

In those days the home run hitter was an oddity. The game was played differently, with clubs scoring runs by using strategy more than brawn. So even though Ruth was about to revolutionize the sport with his extraordinary power, and more and more players would begin copying his swing, he still had his critics—especially those who felt the home run had no place in the game.

The Red Sox found the going tough in 1919 and dropped to sixth place. It was the White Sox, with many of the same players responsible for winning the 1917 World Series, who established themselves as the best in the league in this first season following the end of World War I. The Chicagoans went on to win the AL flag but lost the World Series to Cincinnati under suspicious circumstances. A year later, eight White Sox players were accused of throwing the Fall Classic and were eventually banned from baseball for life by Commissioner Kenesaw Mountain Landis.

Because of the "Black Sox" scandal, history views 1919 as a dark period in baseball. But during that season the American League was being turned upside down by the Babe's home run exploits. His power barrage shocked AL pitchers as he proceeded to set his sights on, then ultimately shatter, all of the single-season home run standards with a record twenty-nine. One by one the previous marks fell:

- The modern AL record of 16 home runs held by "Socks" Seybold of the 1902 Philadelphia Athletics.

- The modern major-league record of 24 held by Gavvy Cravath of the 1915 Philadelphia Phillies.
- The all-time season output of 27, set by Ed Williamson of the Chicago Colts in 1884.

While Ruth was hitting his way to the top and gaining more confidence with each blow, the Red Sox continued to be a sorry franchise. Owner Harry Frazee, who had been losing money on one Broadway show production after another, lost interest in the Boston ballclub and began selling off his players for much-needed capital. In addition, he knew full well he could not meet Ruth's future demands (Babe made $7,000 in 1918 and $10,000 in 1919), which would be astronomical after his exceptional season.

HIGHLIGHTS AND
KEY STATISTICS: 1918–1919

In 1918, Ruth was a potent force both at bat and on the pitching mound. He finished the year with a major-league-leading 11 homers (tied with Tilly Walker of the A's), his first home run title, and, as a hurler, claimed 13 victories with a 2.22 earned run average.

In addition to his record 29 homers, Ruth drove in 114 runs (a major-league high) in 1919. He also belted an unprecedented 4 grand slams, which remained an AL record for forty years.

In light of all this, Frazee was willing to part with his biggest star. The Yankees, then a franchise known for its mediocrity and without a pennant in their history, were being rebuilt by their owners, Colonels Jacob (Jake) Ruppert and Tillinghast L'Hommedieu Huston. These two men, who in the next few years would acquire many top Red Sox players, showed interest in Ruth. The Red Sox finally sold the mighty Babe to New York for an unprecedented sum of $100,000 in cash plus a $300,000 loan.

Babe, in California playing a series of exhibition games, got the word from Yankee manager Miller Huggins. He was surprised but vowed that he would play just as hard for his new team as he had for Boston.

Hindsight shows us that Frazee's financially motivated deal was a huge mistake and probably the worst transaction in baseball history. Babe Ruth helped turn the Yankees into the greatest baseball dynasty of all time, while the Red Sox, over the next seven decades, would fail to capture another world title.

Chapter **5**

RUTH AND
NEW YORK:
A PERFECT
COMBINATION

Babe Ruth's charismatic presence and love of being the center of attention, combined with the excitement and energy of New York and the beginning of the uninhibited "Roaring '20s," made for a perfect match from the very beginning. Babe had been the talk of baseball since 1919, but his popularity really skyrocketed after he came to New York—to such an extent, in fact, that he had to hire sportswriter and cartoonist Christy Walsh to handle his business affairs for him and help him keep his liberal spending to a minimum.

The fans, of course, greeted Babe enthusiastically. They flooded him with fan mail and gifts. It got to the point that a special pay phone had to be installed in the Yankee clubhouse just to handle Babe's calls.

Various ethnic groups around the city adopted him as their own. Italian fans, for example, began calling him "the Bambino," which means *babe* or *baby* in Italian. Sportswriters eventually picked up on this nickname and often used it themselves to refer to Ruth.

But through it all, Babe stayed the same person he'd always been, making time for his many well-wishers, especially the kids.

The acquisition of the game's new "Sultan of Swat" (another nickname Babe would later acquire) was a tremendous boon to the Yankees, who had been nothing more than a weak, second-division club for years. This was in direct contrast to the "other" team that occupied the Polo Grounds, manager John McGraw's Giants, one of baseball's most successful teams.

Colonels Ruppert and Huston, who had purchased the Yankees in 1915, paid a great deal of money for Ruth. They even raised his salary to a whopping $20,000, as Babe—who always felt he deserved the big money and fought hard to get it—began to set the standard for major-league salaries. The two men felt that Ruth was well worth the price and that the prized slugger was the ingredient they needed to reach their goal of winning the AL pennant.

* * * * *

The Yankees of 1919 had finished a close third behind the White Sox and Indians and entered 1920 with the nucleus of an outstanding club. Their lineup was already being called "Murderers' Row" and included such talents as third baseman Frank "Home Run" Baker, first baseman Wally Pipp, and shortstop Roger Peckinpaugh. With Ruth's potent bat in the lineup, aided by what was considered a more lively ball, there was no telling how explosive an offense the Yankees could have. And Ruth, a fun-loving practical joker who was popular with the players throughout his career, fit in perfectly with his teammates.

It didn't take long before Babe, known to his mates as "Jidge" (a slang nickname taken from his real first name), made an impact on the Yankees and dispelled any doubts that he would be able to equal his milestone home run output of 1919. By mid-season, as the Yankees starting

rightfielder, he had surpassed his own "unapproachable" record of twenty-nine, and by the end of the season he had hit an unbelievable fifty-four. Interestingly, he alone out-homered fourteen of the fifteen other teams in baseball.

One of only three players who had a higher batting average than Babe in 1920 was "Shoeless Joe" Jackson, who still has the third best all-time batting average with his career .356 mark. He was also the man who served as Ruth's chief role model.

"I looked for a hitter to copy after," Babe said. "[Ty] Cobb, [Tris] Speaker and [Eddie] Collins weren't my type of hitters, but Jackson had the smoothest, easiest swing of any hitter in the league. So I watched his every action whenever our clubs would meet, and copied it as much as possible. Imitating Joe made me a great hitter."[1]

As fate would have it, the names of Jackson and Ruth would become entwined that year in another way. It was near the conclusion of the 1920 season that the eight White Sox players, of which Jackson was one, were finally exposed. Babe's only connection with the "Black Sox" scandal was that his home run hitting wiped the negative news of the scandal off the front pages. In other times such a scandal might well have done permanent harm to the game. But Ruth's heroics turned America's attention to the game itself and, along with the livelier ball and an upbeat postwar feeling, helped baseball to gain great popularity with people from all walks of life.

"If my home run hitting in 1920 established a new era in baseball, helped the fans of the nation, young and old,

Clouting another homer for the Yankees in 1920 at the Polo Grounds

forget the past and the terrible fact they had been sold out, that's all the epitaph I want.''[2] And of all his contributions to baseball, this undoubtedly was the most significant.

The Yankees, on the strength of Ruth's performance, finished in third place that year, only three games behind first-place Cleveland, as they played before record crowds. Although the Yanks' ultimate goal hadn't yet been reached, the AL pennant was not far away.

* * * * *

All of the optimism created by the Yankees in 1920 was fulfilled in 1921 when the New Yorkers, with Babe enjoying perhaps the greatest single season of all time, won their first AL pennant. Ruth was simply spectacular as he helped the once inept Yankees to ninety-eight victories en route to dethroning the Indians.

In defiance of his many skeptics, who felt that his fifty-four homers the year before were a fluke and that he wouldn't come close to that total again, Ruth slugged fifty-nine that year. This was thirty-five more than the closest competitor. Ruth also broke Roger Connor's career home run mark of 136 and was quickly becoming legendary for his hitting feats, accomplished with his uncommonly large bat.

For example, up until that time no one had ever hit a homer into the centerfield seats at the Polo Grounds. During 1921, Babe walloped not one but two, on consecutive days, with both carrying over 400 feet (120 m). And in a crucial game down the stretch with Cleveland, he pounded two homers, a double, and drove in four runs for an 8–7 Yankee triumph to assure New York the pennant.

Even his high strikeout total and frequent walks (he still holds the career major-league record of 2,056 walks), which come with the territory of being a slugger, had a special excitement all their own. Fans couldn't get enough of seeing Babe come to bat.

The World Series of 1921 was special in that the two teams who were in it—the Yankees and the Giants—played in the same ballpark. However, despite the Yanks' newfound respect, they still were the tenants of the Polo Grounds and second-class citizens to McGraw's powerful Giants, who owned the stadium and also happened to be diehard opponents of the use of the home run, the key to the Yankee attack.

The Yankees still might have won the series if Babe, who hit .313 and the first of fifteen World Series homers in the first five games, hadn't injured his elbow and been forced to sit out the remainder of the classic. It was even more disappointing that in Games 7 and 8 (the Series was best-of-nine that year), Yankee pitchers Carl Mays and Waite Hoyt lost 2–1 and 1–0 heartbreakers. Ruth's bat, most thought, would surely have made the difference.

Despite the World Series defeat, Babe was still the toast of the town. But he also was becoming known for his stunts off the field and his defiance of authority. In fact, following the monumental 1921 season Babe and several other Yankees, including slugger Bob Meusel, took off on a barnstorming trip, playing exhibition games in a number of cities, despite warnings from Baseball Commissioner Landis. As a result, Babe and the others were given suspensions and weren't allowed to return to action until May 20 of the 1922 season.

* * * * *

Despite being named Yankee captain and sporting an astronomical five-year, $52,000 contract, Babe was not the same player in 1922. His suspension was lifted on May 20, but he never quite recovered his form that year. He was in poor physical condition from his fast lifestyle and had continuing problems with his temper, which resulted in even more suspensions that season.

His temper, in fact, got Ruth into hot water early that year when he was thrown out of a game for arguing with an umpire. In addition to the ejection and a heavy fine, he was also removed as captain of the club, a result of his frequent arguments with manager Huggins. However, the Yankees, even with Ruth's problems and his diminished offensive production, were still good enough to beat the St. Louis Browns by one game to win the pennant for the second year in a row.

It was also during that season that Browns' pitcher Hub "Shucks" Pruett forever carved his niche in baseball history at Babe's expense. Pruett, who had a less-than-mediocre major-league mark of 29–48 with four different teams, struck out Ruth ten of the first fourteen times he faced him that year and thirteen of the first twenty-one trips extending into 1923. Ruth's lifetime average against Pruett was below .200. In later years, after Pruett had established himself as a respected doctor in St. Louis, he met up with Babe again.

"I want to thank you for putting me through medical school," Pruett remarked, referring to the fact that his major-league career was lengthened due to his success against Babe. "If it weren't for you, nobody would have ever heard of me."[3] A good-natured Ruth seemed genuinely glad to hear of his former nemesis' good fortune.

HIGHLIGHTS AND
KEY STATISTICS: 1922

This was a subpar season for Babe, as his offensive totals dipped to 35 homers, 99 RBIs, and a .315 batting average. These were very respectable figures for most, but far below Ruth's usual standard of play.

If the regular season was a disaster for Ruth, the World Series that fall against the Giants for the second year in a row was even worse. The combination of McGraw's method of pitching him (a steady diet of low, outside curve balls) and an edict to his players that they should razz the Babe, proved too much. Ruth hit only .118 as the Yankees lost four straight games to their city rivals.

The seemingly invincible Ruth was now being criticized in all quarters, from the man in the street to future New York City Mayor Jimmy Walker, who went on record as saying that Babe Ruth had let down all the kids who looked up to him. There was really nothing Ruth could do about his terrible season, except to vow that he'd be back on top in 1923.

* * * * *

Babe's promise to regain his form was not just talk. Embarrassed by his bad performance in 1922, he trained hard during the off-season, and when the 1923 season started, he was ready to go.

The 1923 season would turn out to be great for Babe and for the club as a whole. Especially memorable was the opening of Yankee Stadium, the longtime dream of Jake Ruppert (now the club's sole owner) who was tired of sharing the Polo Grounds with the rival Giants.

At the stadium's historic opening, on April 18, 1923, 75,000 fans crammed into the new ballpark to see their team battle the Boston Red Sox. Appropriately, it was Babe who rose to the occasion by socking the first home run ever at Yankee Stadium, called "The House That Ruth Built" because of the Bambino's role in the Yankee's success.

"I hit a few more in there during the next twelve years I played in New York," said Babe, who led the Yanks to a convincing 4–1 triumph that day. "Kids will be hitting them when I'm gone, but I'm kind of glad I hit the first one."[4]

That home run, hit into the area of the rightfield stands that would come to be known as "Ruthville," was just one of Babe's big moments that season. In some respects, it was his finest season.

On the basis of his offensive output and the stellar Yankee pitching, New York was the runaway winner in the American League. They overwhelmed the second-place Detroit Tigers by sixteen full games.

The Yankees, who had bowed to McGraw's Giants in the past two World Series, turned the tables in 1923, capturing their first world crown. As anticipated, Ruth was sensational, batting .368 with three home runs, two of them coming in the Yanks' 4–2 victory in Game 2 to even the series at one game each.

Babe was back and voted the unanimous winner of the league's Most Valuable Player award. He had promised a return to the excellence he was long identified with, and he came through with flying colors. It was no surprise that a familiar slogan around baseball was: "As Ruth goes, so go the Yankees."[5]

* * * * *

When Ruth and his teammates came to camp in the spring of 1924, they were aiming to become the first AL team to win four consecutive flags. But though Babe did his part by enjoying another productive season, it was not to be. The 1924 season was the year of "boy manager" Bucky Harris and his Washington Senators. The twenty-seven-year-old skipper led his club to the title by a slim two-game margin over New York.

By 1924, Babe was highly scrutinized wherever he went. He was even given a physical exam by Columbia University, which determined what everyone else knew: that George Herman Ruth was an exceptional physical phenomenon. The study concluded that Ruth scored more than 90 percent in all-around coordination; only one person in six had better eyesight and hearing, and only one in five hundred had better "nervous stability."

HIGHLIGHTS AND
KEY STATISTICS: 1923–1924

Babe certainly rebounded from his "off" year in 1922. During the 1923 season, he increased his batting average 78 points to .393 (his career high); boosted his home run total to 41, which tied for the major-league lead; drew a major-league record 170 walks (a mark that still stands); and had career highs in base hits (205) and doubles (45).

1924 was the only year that Ruth won the AL batting crown, with a .378 average. He also led the majors in several categories, including home runs (46) and runs scored (143).

Left: *playing sensationally during
the 1923 World Series, Babe slides
safely into third base after hitting
a triple. Above: he tips his hat to
the fans after belting a home run.*

Along with his extraordinary physical condition and natural ability, Babe—like so many other ballplayers through the years—was extremely superstitious. He carried a silver dollar as his good luck charm; a white or yellow butterfly meant something to him, but the meaning varied from day to day; he'd go in a hotel through the same door he went out, except if he'd had a bad day—then he'd go in another door. And if he had a good day hunting frogs, a favorite pastime, it meant he would be a success at the plate the next day.

It seemed Ruth had extrasensory perception, too. During a game at Chicago's Comiskey Park, the Yankees' Herb Pennock and the Sox's Mike Cvengros were locked up in a tense pitchers' duel. With the game running late, Yankee traveling secretary Mark Roth nervously reminded Miller Huggins that the club would miss their train if the game didn't end soon. Overhearing the conversation, Babe, the next batter, said, "Don't worry, Mark. We'll make that train. I'll fix that."[6] And he did, smashing a game-winning homer to win the contest moments later!

Chapter 6

THE FALL FROM GRACE AND BACK AGAIN

The good life proved to be too much for baseball's greatest slugger, as Ruth found it hard to resist the temptations in his path, such as food, drink, and staying up all night. His habits were becoming legendary.

For example, Babe once told a teammate his daily breakfast was a pint of whiskey mixed with a pint of ginger ale in a pitcher of ice, followed by a porterhouse steak, four fried eggs, fried potatoes, and a pot of coffee. As far as his late-night activities were concerned, Yankee teammate Ping Bodie was once asked what it was like rooming with Ruth on the road. He replied that he really didn't know, that he roomed with Ruth's suitcase.

As a result of this lifestyle, Babe began 1925 overweight, out of shape, and a constant source of trouble for manager Huggins. Ruth's real troubles started when he fell ill during a series of exhibition games the Yankees were playing on their way north from training camp. Although he got up off his sickbed (so he wouldn't disappoint the fans) to hit two of his longest home runs ever in a game at Chattanooga, Tennessee, Babe continued to run a fever and have stomach problems, eventually resulting in his being hospitalized from April 9 to May 26.

Even when he did return to the lineup, he wasn't the same as before and at the age of thirty was on his way to a below-average season. Some people were convinced his career was over.

His famous "stomach ache," however, wasn't the only problem for Babe that year. He also became involved in a number of serious disputes with Huggins, including one that occurred right before the start of an August game in St. Louis. Ruth arrived at the clubhouse late that day—a common occurrence.

"Don't bother getting dressed, Babe," the skipper told Ruth. "You're not playing today. . . . I'm suspending you and I'm fining you $5,000. You're going back to New York on the five o'clock train. . . ."[1]

Babe was outraged and shouted obscenities at Huggins, making reference to the manager's small stature (5 feet 7 inches, or 1.8 m). Responding to Ruth's outburst, Huggins replied, "Before you get back in uniform, you're going to have to apologize for what you've said. . . ."[2]

Ruth then stormed out of the locker room and headed back to New York, believing that there was no way Miller Huggins could do this to him, the greatest star in baseball. But when he pleaded his case to Colonel Ruppert and asked to be reinstated, he was given a definite "no" and told that Huggins was the boss.

For the next ten days Ruth sat on the sidelines stewing. But, finally, he realized he had been wrong and apologized to the manager. And he never fought with "Hug" again.

"I'm not proud of this," Babe said, referring to the latest of his frequent disputes with Huggins. "It is one of those things a man would like to change if he could alter the past. But men and boys learn from experience and I believe I learned from this one."[3]

*Manager Miller Huggins and
Babe Ruth. Despite their differences,
they respected each other.*

Babe's forgettable season demoralized the Yankee team's pennant hopes, as the New Yorkers dropped to seventh place. In addition to Ruth's off-year, other players were disappointing as well. Joe Dugan was injured for much of the season, and key players of years past, such as shortstop Everett Scott, were at the tail end of their careers.

Perhaps the most significant event of the season occurred in June, when veteran first baseman Wally Pipp complained of a headache and was replaced in the lineup by a youngster named Lou Gehrig. Although Gehrig didn't set the world on fire until a couple of years later, Pipp's troubles enabled Gehrig to become the regular first baseman and ultimately establish the longest consecutive playing streak (2,130 games) in the game's annals.

Not surprisingly, there were many questions about Ruth after the 1925 season. Was his career over? Could the Yankees do without him? Could he make another comeback?

* * * * *

"I admire a man who can win over a lot of tough opponents, but I admire even more a man who can win over himself."[4]

These were the words of Miller Huggins after seeing a new and inspired Babe Ruth in 1926. Ruth, who had an enormous amount of pride, had set out to make good on a promise he had made to redeem himself after his disastrous 1925 season. During the off-season he dedicated himself to getting back into shape, by working out at a New York gym doing all kinds of exercises, and, as in every off-season, spending time outdoors playing golf, hunting, and fishing.

It worked. Babe enjoyed an outstanding summer of baseball in 1926. The Yankees as a team were also revitalized. Rebounding from their dismal next-to-last-place standing, they got off to a strong start and wound up with

baseball's best winning percentage during the regular season. Although Babe was the Yanks' heart, soul, and main offensive weapon, he had an outstanding supporting cast, including Bob Meusel, Earle Combs, a healthy Joe Dugan, first baseman Lou Gehrig (who was making great strides with Ruth's help), and future Hall of Fame pitchers Herb Pennock and Waite Hoyt.

In the World Series that year the Yanks went up against the St. Louis Cardinals, a club led by future Hall of Fame second baseman Rogers Hornsby, who doubled as the Cards' field manager. It was a hard-fought series that came down to the ninth inning of the seventh game. However, it was not a happy outcome for New York, as the Cards won their first World Series.

Baseball historians remember the 1926 series best for the spectacular performance of thirty-nine-year-old pitcher Grover Cleveland Alexander. Although Alexander remains the primary hero of the series, Ruth made a crucial mistake during it that will also long be remembered—perhaps even more than his record three home runs in the fourth game, which led the Yankees to a 10–5 victory and evened the classic at two games apiece.

The Ruth incident happened in the final inning of the last game. With Combs and Koenig retired on groundouts, Babe walked—his record eleventh base on balls of the series—giving Bob Meusel a shot at knocking in the tying run. Meusel, however, never got a chance as Babe, totally on his own, tried to steal second base. Unfortunately for New York, he was thrown out, ending both the game and the hopes of New York for a comeback. After the game

*Ruth with his daughter
Dorothy before the start
of a game in 1926*

Yankees' general manager Ed Barrow told Ruth it was the only dumb play he had ever seen him make.

HIGHLIGHTS AND
KEY STATISTICS: 1925–1926

With all of his personal problems in 1925, Ruth's totals dipped to 25 home runs, 66 runs batted in, and a .290 batting average.

In 1926 Babe made a comeback by batting .372, only 6 percentage points behind the major-league leader, and was the big-league pacesetter in both home runs (47) and RBIs (145). In fact, Babe was the AL home run leader, or co-leader, from 1926 to 1931 and led the majors in all but 1930.

There was nothing dumb, however, about Babe's love of children, his knack of being able to inspire kids everywhere, and his frequent, often unpublicized visits to hospitals and orphanages. It was during the 1926 World Series that his special feeling for youngsters really became a legend, thanks to his relationship with an eleven-year-old New Jersey boy named Johnny Sylvester.

It all began when Johnny Sylvester developed a serious bone disease as a result of a horseback riding accident. In an attempt to lift the boy's spirits, an employee of Johnny's father arranged for both the Yankees and Cardinals to send the youngster autographed baseballs before the start of the World Series. There was also a special message from Ruth himself. It read: "I'll hit a home run for you in Wednesday's game," which was Game 4 in St. Louis.[5] And, unbelievably, it was on that day that Babe hit his record three home runs, one of which was a mammoth effort, perhaps one of the longest ever hit at Sportsman's Park.

Two weeks after the series was over, Ruth paid a visit to Johnny. Babe said, "I thought his eyes would pop out of his head."[6]

Twenty-one years later, Johnny Sylvester would repay the kind gesture by making a special visit to cheer up a dying Babe Ruth.

Chapter 7

THE GREATEST
EVER

Despite the Yankees' failure to win the World Series, the 1926 season was good news for both Babe and the Yanks as they propelled themselves back onto center stage. This was the peak of the Roaring '20s and the Golden Age of sports in the United States, with such heroes as boxer Jack Dempsey, golfer Bobby Jones, and swimmer Johnny Weissmuller grabbing the country's sports spotlight. But it was the carefree Ruth, the slugger who perhaps received more publicity than even the president, who was the nation's foremost sports personality. And, in turn, the Yankees were its most revered team.

Despite their rise to prominence in 1926, no one could have predicted that by the time the 1927 season was over, this club would have established itself as "The Greatest Team Ever." And Babe himself would have recorded one of the most memorable records in sports history by hitting sixty home runs.

There have been many great teams in baseball, but the 1927 Yankees are considered, by many experts, to have been the best club ever, even to this day. They won

110 games, finished nineteen games ahead of the second-place Philadelphia A's (who were stocked with such Hall of Fame talent as Ty Cobb, Mickey Cochrane, Jimmie Foxx, and Lefty Grove), and led the major leagues in several categories, including home runs, team batting average, and earned run average for pitchers.

"When we were challenged, when we had to win, we stuck together and played with a fury and a determination that could come only from team spirit," standout pitcher Waite Hoyt once said. "We had pride in our performance that was very real. It took on the form of snobbery. We felt we were superior people, and I do believe we left a heritage that became a Yankee tradition."[1] Manager Miller Huggins summed it up by stating that his was the only team in history that didn't need the breaks.

The Yankees' winning ways continued into the World Series, where they faced a fine Pittsburgh Pirates team featuring Hall of Fame performers Paul and Lloyd Waner, Pie Traynor, and Kiki Cuyler. It was apparent from the outset, however, that the Yanks would dominate. They proceeded to sweep the Pirates, 5–4, 6–2, 8–1, and 4–3. Carrying over his red-hot hitting from the regular season, Babe led the way in the World Series with a pair of homers, 7 RBIs, and a .400 batting average.

Along with winning the world title, the most exciting part of the 1927 season was Babe's assault on his own home run record. It had been six years since Ruth had walloped his career high of fifty-nine in 1921. Many experts were saying he would never hit sixty. But from the time the thirty-two-year-old Ruth got to spring training, in excellent shape and delighted with a new three-year $70,000 contract, it looked like he was destined for an extraordinary year.

After hitting just four homers in April, Ruth slugged his way through May, hitting twelve more. He was as consistent as he could be during the next three months, hitting nine home runs each in June, July, and August (including

two home runs each in four different games). One of his most memorable homers was in mid-August, when he became the first player ever to hit a ball over the rightfield stands in Chicago's Comiskey Park.

Ruth had hit forty-three homers going into the final month of the season. By this time, baseball fans everywhere were closely watching Babe's quest, as well as his hitting duel with teammate Lou Gehrig, who was just two home runs behind at that stage. The Ruth-Gehrig battle ended, however, as Lou dropped off the pace. Babe, despite the coolness he and Gehrig felt for each other in later years, always said that he would never have set the record without Gehrig hitting behind him in the fourth slot in the batting order.

With forty-three down and a sizable seventeen to go, Ruth began his September with a long homer against the Philadelphia A's, the 400th of his career. On September 6, he hit three in a doubleheader against the Red Sox and added two more the next day to reach forty-nine. Number fifty came four days later, and numbers fifty-one and fifty-two were hit on September 13, the day the Yankees clinched their fifth AL flag in seven years.

In the next two weeks, Babe hit five more, to bring him to fifty-seven, and on September 29, he hit a pair—one a grand slam—to defeat the Washington Senators. He was now one homer away from the elusive sixty mark, with two days remaining in the season.

Ruth didn't wait quite until the "eleventh hour." On Friday, September 30, the second to the last day of the 154-game schedule, he etched his name in the record books with number sixty—a two-run shot off Senators' pitcher Tom Zachary that won the ball game.

Lou Gehrig and Babe Ruth

Above: *hitting his 60th home run in 1927
to break the season home-run record.*
Right: *Lou Gehrig (with bat) greets
Babe at the plate to congratulate him.*

"It was not necessary to follow the course of the ball," *The New York Times* reported the following day. "The boys in the bleachers indicated the route of the record homer . . . a fitting wallop to top the Babe's 59 in 1921."

"While the crowd cheered and the Yankee players roared their greeting, the Babe made his triumphant, almost regal tour of the paths. He jogged around slowly, touched each base firmly and carefully and when he imbedded his spikes into the rubber dish [home plate] . . . hats were tossed liberally and the spirit of celebration permeated the place."[2]

It was a fitting conclusion to a dream year—the record stood until 1961, when the Yankees' Roger Maris surpassed it with sixty-one in a 162-game season.

HIGHLIGHTS AND
KEY STATISTICS: 1927

Aside from the Yankees' overall team success, the New Yorkers were remarkable individually as well. Babe swatted his record home run total, 60, along with 164 RBIs and a .356 batting mark. Gehrig, who really came into his own to firmly establish him and Ruth as the greatest 1-2 punch baseball has ever known, clubbed 47 home runs, with a major-league-leading 175 RBIs and a .373 batting average. Other chief contributors included Bob Meusel (.337 average and 103 RBIs), Tony Lazzeri (18 homers, 102 RBIs), and Earle Combs (.356 average). On the mound Waite Hoyt led the way with a 22–7 mark, followed by Wilcy Moore (19–7), Herb Pennock (19–8), and Urban Shocker (18–6).

How could Babe and the Yankees top 1927? They couldn't, but the Yanks, with the same nucleus of players from the year before, still emerged as baseball's best team in 1928, with 101 victories in a tight race with Philadelphia and a four-game sweep of the Cardinals in the World Series. During the series, and in spite of a bad leg, Babe Ruth was magnificent, setting a series record that still stands by hitting a sizzling .625 and slugging three homers in a single game for the second time in series play. The second of his three homers in Game 4 ranks as one of the most remarkable of an already remarkable career.

HIGHLIGHTS AND
KEY STATISTICS: 1928

Babe followed his 60-homer season with a major-league-leading 54 roundtrippers and drove in 142 runs, tying Gehrig for the big-league lead. Between the two sluggers, they hit 81 home runs, drove across 284 runs, scored more than 300 times, and averaged close to .350.

It was in the seventh inning when Babe, who had hit his first homer of the day in the fourth inning, stepped up to the plate against Bill Sherdel. St. Louis was ahead 2–1. There was one out. Sherdel got two strikes on Ruth and then tossed a "quick pitch" to catch Babe by surprise. It would have been the third strike, but that type of pitch, legal in the National League, was against AL rules. After a long argument it was decided that Sherdel would have to make the pitch over.

This was not good news for St. Louis, as Babe, in his usual dramatic fashion, proceeded to smack home run number two into the rightfield stands to tie the score. Moments later, Gehrig also smashed a home run, to put the Yankees in the lead for good. In the ninth inning, Ruth hit his third homer of the game.

During the off-season, as they had in the past, Ruth and Gehrig capitalized on their triumphs and played in a series of exhibition games around the country. It was certainly the best of times for Babe Ruth and the New York Yankees.

Chapter

8

A TIME OF TRANSITION

Following their near-perfect seasons of 1927 and 1928, Ruth and the Yankees came down to earth in 1929, experiencing their share of highs and lows.

On a personal level, Babe was deeply saddened by the death of his wife, Helen, who was killed in a house fire. Even though they had been separated for years, Ruth had a special feeling for her and their foster daughter Dorothy. Months later, however, things got better for Babe on the homefront, when he married longtime friend Claire Merritt Hodgson, and the couple eventually adopted both Dorothy and Claire's daughter, Julia.

Claire, a native of Athens, Georgia, was an attractive New York chorus girl when she met Babe. Not long after their first meeting, the two fell in love. When Babe separated from Helen, Claire and Julia moved in with him. Although Ruth and Helen had been unhappy together for a long time, Babe, who was Catholic, would not get a divorce.

Claire was a good influence on her husband. She served him nutritious meals and persuaded him to cut

Babe with his second wife,
Claire, and daughter Julia

down on his drinking and carefree spending. Whereas Helen had been quiet and unassuming, Claire was worldly, outgoing, and strong. Their marriage of almost twenty years seemed to be a very happy one.

On the field, Ruth wore his legendary number 3 (which was later retired) for the first time as the Yankees began putting numbers on uniforms. Although he had some minor injuries, they didn't seriously disrupt his play, and he had another terrific year. However, the Yankees were unable to repeat their successes of the two previous seasons. Owner-manager Connie Mack's Philadelphia A's proved to be too much for New York, which finished eighteen games behind in second place.

Another sad event occurred in 1929. On September 25, just before the end of the season, Miller Huggins died at the age of fifty. Babe had grown to respect deeply the diminutive skipper after their early run-ins and felt a real loss for the man who had won six pennants and three World Series titles in the decade of the '20s.

Although he was saddened by Huggins' death, Babe let it be known that he wanted to be the next Yankee manager. Ruth, who felt he was the ideal choice, reasoned that he had been in baseball for sixteen years and with the Yankees for ten, and that he had played a few different positions and therefore knew the game. He also pointed to the fact that many of his superstar colleagues, such as Ty Cobb, Tris Speaker, Rogers Hornsby, Eddie Collins, and Ray Schalk, all got a crack at managing.

Babe's plea, though, fell upon deaf ears, with Jake Ruppert saying, "You can't manage yourself, how do you expect to manage others?"[1] A few days later, Ruth's teammate Bob Shawkey was given the job.

Ruth began 1930 with a record contract of $80,000. When someone mentioned that he was making more than the president of the United States, Babe simply said, "Why not? I had a better year than he did."[2]

Ruth continued his outstanding play in 1930, but

Children watch in awe as an
official of the Baseball Hall of
Fame in Cooperstown, New York,
proudly places Babe's uniform in a
display case for all to admire.

despite this the Yanks fell to third place behind the powerful A's and Washington Senators. With the exception of the disaster of 1925, it was the Yankees' worst season since 1920. Not surprisingly, Shawkey was fired as manager after the season. Again, Babe made a pitch for the job; again, Ruppert turned him down. When the 1931 season began, Joe McCarthy, former manager of the Cubs, was the new Yankee manager.

McCarthy's presence improved the club, which finished the year second to the A's in the final standings. But Ruth didn't get along with McCarthy, probably partly because he had the job Ruth wanted. As Babe prepared for the 1932 season, he could never have suspected that it would be such a landmark season for both him and the Yankees—and that he would play in his tenth and final World Series.

HIGHLIGHTS AND
KEY STATISTICS: 1929–1931

The Bambino led both leagues in 1929 with 46 home runs along with 154 RBIs and a .345 batting mark.

In 1930, at the age of 35, Ruth led the American League with 49 homers while driving in 153 runs with a .359 batting average.

The amazing duo of Ruth and Gehrig continued to pound AL pitching during the 1931 season. Babe socked 46 homers with 163 RBIs and a .373 average, second in the majors. Lou clubbed an identical number of home runs with 184 RBIs and a .341 mark. The two Yankee immortals shared the major-league home run title.

After two years of earning his maximum salary of $80,000, Ruth began 1932 with a $5,000 pay cut. It wasn't that his game had deteriorated; it was simply a sign of the times. This was the height of the Great Depression, and everyone had to do their part, even Babe Ruth.

The money may have been down, but the Yankees were up, and after a great start they easily won the AL pennant. Babe's contributions that year were outstanding as were the performances of a new generation of Yankee stars, such as pitchers Lefty Gomez and Red Ruffing and catcher Bill Dickey. All were eventually elected to the Hall of Fame.

In the 1932 World Series the Yankees faced McCarthy's old club, the Cubs. The New Yorkers won four straight games, giving them the distinction of sweeping twelve consecutive World Series contests over three different clubs (Pirates, Cardinals, and Cubs).

That Fall Classic is also one of the most talked about in baseball history. And, like so many other unforgettable events, Babe was in the middle of it, this time because of his fabled "Called Shot."

In Games 1 and 2 at Yankee Stadium, the Yankees won amidst a great deal of bad feeling between the two clubs, aggravated by an incident concerning former Yankee Mark Koenig, who had joined the Cubs from the minor leagues mid-season and had been voted only a half-share of World Series money. During the games there was a lot of bench-jockeying back and forth, some of it vicious.

When the two teams traveled to Chicago for Game 3, they found the fans there already stirred up by the publicity. Among the angriest of all the Yanks was Ruth, who vowed: "I'll belt one where it hurts most." He got his chance during the fifth inning of the third game at Wrigley Field. Here is how Babe recalled the controversial "Called Shot" in his autobiography:

My ears had been blistered so much before in my baseball career that I thought they had lost all feeling. But the blast was turned on me by Cub players and some of the fans penetrated and cut deep. Some of the fans started throwing vegetables at me.

I stepped back out of the box, then stepped in. And while [pitcher] Charlie Root was getting ready to throw his first pitch, I pointed to the bleachers which rise out of deep centerfield.

Root threw one right across the gut of the plate and I let it go. But before the umpire could call it a strike, which it was, I raised my right hand, stuck out one finger and yelled, "Strike one." The razzing was stepped up a notch.

Root got set and threw again, another hard one through the middle. And once again I stepped back and held up my right hand and bawled, "Strike two!" It was.

You should have heard those fans then. As for the Cub players, they came out on the steps of the dugout and really let me have it. I guess the smart thing for Charlie to have done on his third pitch would have been to waste one. But he didn't, and for that I've sometimes thanked God.

While he was making up his mind to pitch to me I stepped back again and pointed my finger at those bleachers, which only caused the mob to howl that much more at me. Root threw me a fastball. If I had let it go, it would have been called a strike. But this was IT. I swung from the ground with everything I had and as I hit the ball, every muscle in my system, every sense I had, told me that I had never hit a better one, that as long as I lived nothing would ever feel as good as this.

I didn't have to look. But I did. That ball just went on and on and on and hit far up in the centerfield bleachers in exactly the same spot I pointed to. To me, it was the funniest, proudest moment I had ever had in baseball. I jogged toward first base, rounded it, looked back at the

*A painting by artist Douglass Crockwell
depicting Ruth's "Called Shot"*

*Cub bench, and suddenly got convulsed with laughter.
You should have seen those Cubs. As [Earle] Combs said
later, "There they were, all out on the top step and yelling
their brains out, and then you connected and they
watched it and then fell back as if they were being
machine gunned."*

*That home run—the most famous one I ever hit—did
us some good. . . .. we won that ball game, 7–5.*[3]

Babe's story changed from time to time, and on occasion
he even denied he ever pointed to the outfield. But the
"Called Shot," whether it was fact or fiction, is one of the
most talked about incidents in sports history, and one of
the reasons Babe Ruth became a legend in his own
time.

HIGHLIGHTS AND
KEY STATISTICS: 1932
Still a premier slugger at 37 years of age, Babe hit
41 homers, drove in 137 runs, and compiled a .341
batting average.

Chapter

9

THE END OF
AN ERA

With the exception of a couple of typically Ruthian performances in the next couple of years, 1932 was Babe's last season as a premier slugger. He was thirty-eight in 1933 and back to the $52,000 salary he had received in the mid-1920s. Understandably, his production at the plate slipped, as he relinquished his leadership role to Gehrig. Sorely missing the old Ruth, the Yankees finished second in a close race with the Washington Senators.

The Ruth magic was not completely gone, however. In the very first All-Star Game, at Comiskey Park in Chicago, Babe appropriately hit the first ever All-Star homer and made a spectacular catch to lead the American Leaguers to a 4–2 victory. The fans should have realized that the great one, despite the wear and tear of twenty big-league seasons, would rise to the occasion.

"Occasions like that have always done something to me," Ruth said of his 1933 All-Star performance. "Maybe ballplayers like myself have a touch of the ham in them, or maybe a touch of the fire horse. But there's something about a big crowd and an event that everybody is watch-

Left to right: *Jimmie Foxx,
Babe Ruth, and Lou Gehrig pose
for the cameras at the 1934 All-Star
game held on July 10, 1934.*

ing or reading about or listening to. Things like that always made me want to do my best."[1]

It was also the year that Babe's dream of managing almost became a reality. Frank Navin, owner of the Detroit Tigers, wanted Ruth to manage his club. Babe, saying the discussions could keep, postponed a meeting with Navin because he had plans to play in a series of exhibition games in Hawaii. Apparently Navin was annoyed by the casual way Ruth treated the proposal, for when Ruth finally arrived on the islands, he learned that the A's star catcher Mickey Cochrane had been signed to manage the club.

* * * * *

The 1934 season was not a good one for Yankee fans, as the club finished seven games out of first place while Cochrane's Tigers won the American League flag. It was also Babe's final season in Yankee pinstripes, and he was struggling. To make matters worse, in the 1934 All-Star Game, he had the dubious distinction of being the first of five future Hall of Famers New York Giant pitcher Carl Hubbell struck out in succession. After disposing of Ruth, "King Carl" made history by striking out Lou Gehrig, Jimmie Foxx, Al Simmons, and Joe Cronin as well.

Following the season, Babe went off to Japan with a group of other major-league stars. The American players—especially Babe—were greeted with wild enthusiasm, and the games were all sold out in expectation of seeing Ruth in action. As usual, Babe rose to the occasion by hitting thirteen home runs in seventeen games. Before going home, the team played in Shanghai and Manila, and following the tour Babe left the group and traveled further, ending up in Paris and London.

After two seasons in decline, Ruth had now outlived his usefulness in New York, and the Yankees were willing to let him go. There were those, however, who felt he still belonged in the majors. And before the 1935 campaign, Judge Emil Fuchs, owner of the National League's Boston Braves, made Ruth a vice-president, assistant manager, and player, allowing Ruth to return to Boston where his major-league career had begun two decades before.

But things didn't work out, and Ruth asked to be relieved of his duties and left the Braves after a road trip early in the season. It was on that trip that Babe exhibited his last bit of magic, getting four hits in four trips to the plate, three home runs, and six RBIs in one game against the Pirates at Pittsburgh's Forbes Field on May 25.

After he hit his third home run of the day in the seventh inning, Ruth left the game as the appreciative fans gave him a standing ovation. Many people said that the blast, which cleared the rightfield grandstand and wound up in a park across the street, was the longest homer ever hit at Forbes Field. Ironically, that home run was his 714th—the final, home run of his career and a record that stood until 1974 when another Brave, Henry (Hank) Aaron of the Atlanta Braves, eclipsed the mark.

HIGHLIGHTS AND
KEY STATISTICS: 1933–1935

Having been able to evade "Father Time" up until 1933, Babe's production finally began to decline. He hit 34 home runs, drove in 103 runs, and dipped to a .301 batting average.

In his final year as a Yankee and his last full season in the major leagues in 1934, Babe hit 22 home runs with 84 RBIs and a .288 batting average in just 125 games.

During 1935, in his last 28 games, Babe hit just .181; appropriately, 6 out of his 13 hits were home runs.

*Babe making his last career
pitching appearance in 1933*

Just a few days later, in Philadelphia, Ruth suffered a knee injury and had to leave the game. It was his last appearance as a major league player. He officially retired a few days later, ending a glorious career in which he had set scores of records, including many that still stand. Among the existing major league records are his .690 career slugging percentage; his all-time home run frequency (a homer every 11.8 times at bat); an unmatched total of twelve league home run titles; and the record seventy-two times he hit two home runs in a single game.

* * * * *

A bitter Ruth, who never got over his disappointment of being denied a chance to manage, retired to the golf course and made a host of public appearances. In 1936 he was one of the five original electees—with Ty Cobb, Honus Wagner, Walter Johnson, and Christy Mathewson—into the National Baseball Hall of Fame in Cooperstown, New York. In mid-season of 1938 the Brooklyn Dodgers offered Babe a coaching job, which he accepted. But he felt out of place. He was just not used to serving in a support role. He had always been the star.

Now out of baseball for good, Babe involved himself in a variety of activities during the next several years. He worked with the Ford Motor Company's American Legion junior baseball program, the Red Cross, and played in several benefit baseball games, including a 1942 contest at Yankee Stadium where he renewed his classic rivalry (which began about twenty-five years earlier) with the great pitcher Walter Johnson, who pitched for the opposing team. He also played himself in the popular movie about Lou Gehrig, *The Pride of the Yankees* (he had dabbled in movies earlier in his career as well) and traveled throughout the world taking advantage of his universal popularity.

Babe certainly kept busy following his retirement, but

at the same time he was plagued by a variety of health problems. In the late 1930s he suffered a mild heart attack and about a year later he had another one. He also had a bout with a bad cold and nervous exhaustion in the early 1940s, and a few years later was hospitalized for a knee operation.

Then in November 1946, Babe experienced some pain over his left eye. At first, it was thought to be nothing more than a sinus headache, but it turned out to be a cancerous growth on the left side of his neck. Despite an operation, which removed most, but not all, of the cancer, the entire left side of Babe's head was affected, including the larynx (which contains the vocal cords). He was hospitalized for three months, then released in February of 1947, at which time he went to Florida for rest and recuperation. Although his release from the hospital was welcome, the outlook wasn't good.

* * * * *

On April 27, 1947, the Yankees staged Babe Ruth Day, similar to the tribute they had given to a dying Lou Gehrig eight years earlier. Babe, with the effects of the cancer visibly apparent both in his body and voice, emotionally addressed the 60,000 fans who gathered to pay him homage at "The House That Ruth Built." In concluding, he said:

Above: *looking over the collection of photographs and cartoons on a wall in his New York apartment shortly after his retirement.* Below: *children at a hospital get the Babe's autograph written in copies of his book,* How to Play Baseball.

The only real game in the world, I think, is baseball. As a rule, some people think if you give them [boys] a football or a baseball or something like that, naturally, they're athletes right away. But you can't do that in baseball. You've got to start from way down, at the bottom, when you're six or seven years old. You can't wait until you're fifteen or sixteen. You've got to let it grow up with you, and if you're successful and you try hard enough, you're bound to come out on top, just like these boys have come to the top now.

There's been so many lovely things said about me, I'm glad I had the opportunity to thank everybody. Thank you.[2]

A little more than a year later, on June 13, 1948, Babe Ruth attended the celebration of Yankee Stadium's twenty-fifth anniversary. He was reunited with Yankee pals Joe Dugan, Bob Meusel, Wally Pipp, Mark Koenig, and others, and despite his worsening physical condition and the constant pain he endured from both his illness and the treatment for it, he enjoyed reliving the old days with his buddies.

Shortly after the anniversary festivities Ruth entered Memorial Hospital in New York City and stayed there, leaving only on special occasions. One of those times was on July 26, when the former slugger and his family went to the premiere of the film *The Babe Ruth Story*, but he was too weak to stay until the end.

Tanned and smiling, Babe and Claire return to New York from a six-week vacation in Florida where he had recuperated after being released from the hospital.

*The great Yankee slugger making
his last appearance in uniform
at Yankee Stadium during its
twenty-fifth anniversary celebration.
Thousands cheered the beloved Babe.*

Three weeks later, on August 16, Babe Ruth, who was never aware of the exact cause of his illness, died. He was fifty-three years old. Millions from around the globe mourned his passing. In New York a funeral mass was held at St. Patrick's Cathedral, and thousands of people of all ages and all walks of life lined up for blocks to pay their final respects to Ruth, who was then appropriately brought to lie in state at Yankee Stadium.

In his life, Babe established himself as perhaps sports' greatest hero. He changed the course of baseball history and was beloved by young and old everywhere. Upon his death he left a remarkable legacy for the ages: He was the best there ever was!

BABE RUTH:
THE STATISTICAL RECORD

BATTING KEY:

G—Games
AB—At Bats
H—Hits
2B—Doubles
3B—Triples
HR—Home Runs
R—Runs
RBI—Runs Batted In
BB—Bases on Balls (Walks)
SO—Strikeouts
SB—Stolen Bases
BA—Batting Average (The number of hits divided by
      the number of at bats.)
SP—Slugging Percentage (The total number of bases
      of all safe hits divided by the total times at bat.)

PITCHING KEY:
W—Wins
L—Losses
PCT—Winning Percentage (The number of games
        won divided by the total number of games
        won and lost.)
ERA—Earned Run Average (The number of earned
        runs multiplied by nine; that number divided
        by the number of innings pitched.)
G—Games
GS—Games Started
CG—Complete Games
IP—Innings Pitched
H—Hits
BB—Bases on Balls (Walks)
SO—Strikeouts
SHO—Shutouts

BATTING

Bold face indicates American League leadership

Source: The Baseball Encyclopedia, Macmillan Publishing Company, Inc.

† Indicates major league single-season record

*Indicates major league career record

		G	AB	H	2B	3B	HR	R	RBI	BB	SO	SB	BA	SP
1914	Red Sox	5	10	2	1	0	0	1	0	0	4	0	.200	.300
1915	Red Sox	42	92	29	10	1	4	16	21	9	23	0	.315	.576
1916	Red Sox	67	136	37	5	3	3	18	16	10	23	0	.272	.419
1917	Red Sox	52	123	40	6	3	2	14	12	12	18	0	.325	.472
1918	Red Sox	95	317	95	26	11	**11**	50	66	57	**58**	6	.300	**.555**
1919	Red Sox	130	432	139	34	12	**29**	**103**	**114**	101	58	7	.322	**.657**
1920	Yankees	142	458	172	36	9	**54**	**158**	**137**	**148**	80	14	.376	†**.847**
1921	Yankees	152	540	204	44	16	**59**	**177**	**171**	**144**	81	17	.378	**.846**
1922	Yankees	110	406	128	24	8	35	94	99	84	80	2	.315	**.672**
1923	Yankees	152	522	205	45	13	**41**	**151**	**131**	**170**	**93**	17	.393	**.764**
1924	Yankees	153	529	200	39	7	**46**	**143**	121	**142**	**81**	9	**.378**	**.739**
1925	Yankees	98	359	104	12	2	25	61	66	59	68	2	.290	.543
1926	Yankees	152	495	184	30	5	**47**	**139**	**145**	**144**	76	11	.372	**.737**
1927	Yankees	151	540	192	29	8	**60**	**158**	**164**	**138**	**89**	7	.356	**.772**
1928	Yankees	154	536	173	29	8	**54**	**163**	**142**	**135**	**87**	4	.323	**.709**
1929	Yankees	135	499	172	26	6	**46**	**121**	154	72	60	5	.345	**.697**
1930	Yankees	145	518	186	28	9	**49**	**150**	153	**136**	61	10	.359	**.732**
1931	Yankees	145	534	199	31	3	**46**	**149**	163	**128**	51	5	.373	**.700**
1932	Yankees	133	457	156	13	5	41	120	137	**130**	62	2	.341	.661
1933	Yankees	137	459	138	21	3	34	97	103	**114**	90	4	.301	.582
1934	Yankees	125	365	105	17	4	22	78	84	103	63	1	.288	.537
1935	Braves	28	72	13	0	0	6	13	12	20	24	0	.181	.431
22 yrs.		2503	8399	2873	506	136	714	2174	2211	*2056	1330	123	.342	*.690
WORLD SERIES 10 yrs.		41	129	42	5	2	15	37	33	33	30	4	.326	.744

PITCHING

Bold face indicates.
American League leadership

Source: The Baseball Encyclopedia, Macmillan Publishing Company, Inc.

		W	L	PCT	ERA	G	GS	CG	IP	H	BB	SO	SHO
1914	**Red Sox**	2	1	.667	3.91	4	3	1	23	21	7	3	0
1915	**Red Sox**	18	8	.692	2.44	32	28	16	217.2	166	85	112	1
1916	**Red Sox**	23	12	.657	**1.75**	44	**41**	23	323.2	230	118	170	**9**
1917	**Red Sox**	24	13	.649	2.01	41	38	**35**	326.1	244	108	128	6
1918	**Red Sox**	13	7	.650	2.22	20	19	18	166.1	125	49	40	1
1919	**Red Sox**	9	5	.643	2.97	17	15	12	133.1	148	58	30	0
1920	**Yankees**	1	0	1.000	4.50	1	1	0	4	3	2	0	0
1921	**Yankees**	2	0	1.000	9.00	2	1	0	9	14	9	2	0
1930	**Yankees**	1	0	1.000	3.00	1	1	1	9	11	2	3	0
1933	**Yankees**	1	0	1.000	5.00	1	1	1	9	12	3	0	0
10 yrs.		94	46	.671	2.28	163	148	107	1221.1	974	441	488	17
WORLD SERIES													
2 yrs.		3	0	1.000	0.87	3	3	2	31	19	10	8	1

Notes

CHAPTER ONE
1. Robert W. Creamer, *Babe* (New York: Simon and Schuster, 1974), 22.
2. Lee Allen, *Babe Ruth: His Story in Baseball* (New York: G. P. Putnam's Sons, 1966), 17.

CHAPTER TWO
1. Babe Ruth with Bob Considine, *The Babe Ruth Story* (New York: E. P. Dutton and Company, Inc., 1948), 12.
2. Ibid., 55–56.
3. Creamer, 37.
4. Ruth with Considine, 17.
5. Anthony J. O'Connor, *Voices From Cooperstown* (New York: Macmillan Publishing Company, 1982), 34.
6. Ruth with Considine, 20–21.
7. Ibid., 21.
8. Creamer, 63.

CHAPTER THREE
1. Lawrence Ritter, *The Glory of Their Times* (New York: Macmillan Publishing Company, 1966), 136–37.
2. Ruth with Considine, 34.

CHAPTER FOUR
1. Creamer, 152.
2. Ruth with Considine, 63.

CHAPTER FIVE
1. Fred Lieb, "Nation Mourns Ruth," *The Sporting News* (August 25, 1948), Sec. 2, 4.
2. Ruth with Considine, 91.
3. Creamer, 267.
4. Ruth with Considine, 126.
5. Ibid.
6. Waite Hoyt, *Babe Ruth as I Knew Him* (New York: Dell Publishing Company, 1948), 21.

CHAPTER SIX
1. Creamer, 292–293.
2. Ibid., 293.
3. Ruth with Considine, 143.
4. Ibid., 147.
5. Brian Sobel, "The True Story of Babe Ruth's Famous Visit to Ailing Youth," *Baseball Digest* (March 1986), 82.
6. Ruth with Considine, 173.

CHAPTER SEVEN
1. John Mosedale, *The Greatest of All* (New York: The Dial Press, 1974), 157.
2. Lowell Reidenbaugh, *Baseball's Greatest Games* (St. Louis: The Sporting News Publishing Company, 1986), 162.

CHAPTER EIGHT
1. Ruth with Considine, 178.
2. Creamer, 351.
3. Ruth with Considine, 193–94.

CHAPTER NINE
1. Ruth with Considine, 199.
2. Creamer, 419.

Further Reading

Creamer, Robert W. *Babe: The Legend Comes to Life.* New York: Simon and Schuster, 1974.

Haskins, James. *Babe Ruth and Hank Aaron: The Home Run Kings.* New York: Lothrop, Lee and Shepard, 1974.

Ruth, Babe with Bob Considine. *The Babe Ruth Story.* New York: E. P. Dutton and Company, 1948.

Smelser, Marshall. *The Life that Ruth Built.* New York: Quadrangle/The New York Times Book Company, 1975.

Smith, Robert. *Babe Ruth's America.* New York: Thomas Y. Crowell Company, 1974.

Sobol, Ken. *Babe Ruth and the American Dream.* New York: Random House, 1974.

Verral, Charles Spain. *Babe Ruth: Sultan of Swat.* Champaign, Illinois: Garrard Publishing Company, 1976.

Index